The Gift of Leadership

How to Coach Your Team to More Productive and Efficient Outcomes

ISBN: 978-0-9884471-9-6

YouSpeakIt
P U B L I S H I N G
The Easy Way
to Get Your Book
Done Right™

www.YouSpeakItPublishing.com

Dedication

This book is dedicated to God and Vivia.

I would truly like to thank these two critically important people in my life.

First, I give all of the Glory to God Almighty, who brought me from the depths of a fairly rugged existence to a place where I started to understand true Love, Grace, Kindness, and Mercy.

And for thirty-five years, my wife, Vivia, has been my rock and partner on this journey. What a wonderful and beautiful gift from God.

Acknowledgments

I would like to thank the following for all of their help in creating this book:

Dave Sloan took a chance on me when I was just a kid and worked to guide me in life and career. In 1987, he set me on this path of leadership and management. He has been coaching me for thirty years and he is still coaching me today.

Thanks also to Ken Blanchard, who told me in 2003 that I should write a book.

Bob Bennett has been a model for lifelong learning.

My Uncle Harry Lintucum has been like a Dad to me.

The Toyota Motor Corporation has allowed me to grow and develop in ways that I would have never been able to do on my own. It has given me a deep foundation to build on.

The Christian Church this has been my family from the time I started seeking God. As we moved our family from state to state, I have found like-minded people who love God and who want to serve Him.

The team at Louis Vuitton helped me understand that there are many ways to birth and grow a company.

And lastly, Keith and Maura Leon of YouSpeakIt Publishing have given tremendous help throughout the process of writing this book. I didn't know where I would start it or where I would end. They made it easy for me.

Table of Contents

Introduction

Throughout the history of my personal journey in leadership, whether in my family, the church, or within organizations, I have benefitted from tools and insights that I want to share with you now in this book.

I was asked to write this book a few times, but I kept turning people down. I didn't know how to write a book. I felt like I was more of a verbal communicator than a writer. Then people much wiser than I, and much stronger in the area of leadership, influenced me to do it. They encouraged me and told me it was something I needed to do. So here it is!

The process of writing brought back a lot of memories. It's like reading a good book in which you kind of already know some of the things that you're reading, but the reading of it reinforces your behaviors, or makes you continue to adjust just enough to make you a little bit better in the process.

When you reflect on your past and write something like this, it forces you to relive a lot of the experiences. It reminds you that these things are critical to your success and the way in which you've been moving throughout this time as a leader. In writing this book, I feel like I've given myself my own history lesson.

You may want to read this book cover to cover, but I'm not really that kind of a reader. I like to pick up a book and think about what I need right now. I open to a chapter that captures me and read it, then maybe move forward or backward from there. To some people, that style probably seems a little bit backwards.

The chapters stand on their own. Depending on your needs and different conditions, you will be able to pull something out of each one.

You will gain knowledge, understanding, and wisdom that you can use to enhance your own leadership skills. This book can improve whatever you're doing in your arena, whether you find yourself leading within the home, community, church, or leading within a business or organization.

My hope is that you will find strong pieces of information that may become best practices for you, that would enhance your ability to lead your team to new heights, and to be more productive and more efficient, and to have more fun in the journey as you lead.

Leadership is tough. Leadership is a lot of work. But it is certainly very rewarding, and has great joy. If you do it well, the rewards are endless and priceless.

CHAPTER
ONE

Communication Tips

BE A GOOD LISTENER AND SEEK TO UNDER-STAND

If you really are going to be able to impact or influence a condition, then you have to foster listening in a way that allows you to truly hear what someone is saying to you. When most folks are listening to someone trying to explain a situation or a condition to them, they're jumping to conclusions. When someone comes to you as the leader, and you assume that you're the authority on a topic, you may hear something that isn't necessarily true. You may assume you know exactly what that person will say or that you already know their question. Instead, you have to figure out how to foster yourself to listen.

The Best Leaders Ask the Best Questions

Most leaders want to share their experience and they want to be able to offer valuable help to someone who is coming to them with a problem, a situation, or a condition. Unless you can assess what's really going on with someone, and what's going on with the situation or the condition, you really can't add any value.

But if you can figure out how to ask the right questions, if you can really concentrate and focus on simple things, you can get to the cause.

Ask the simple questions, like:

Who . . . ?
What . . . ?
Where . . . ?
When . . . ?
Why . . . ?

Throughout my life, I've learned that it takes about five times of asking why to discover a root cause or a root condition.

It's like when someone notices the light isn't working in a room. They change the light bulb, and two days later, their light goes out again. They replace it again.

They just keep changing the light bulb instead of asking, "*Why* are we having that problem?"

An electrician would ask questions. Maybe the root cause is way down the line. For instance:

Is the problem really with the light bulb?

Maybe it's the ballast.

Well, is it the ballast?

That's the question. We don't know. Maybe it's the next thing up the line. Maybe it's a circuit breaker that's bad.

Why has the circuit breaker gone bad?

It may have gone bad because there's a bad utility box in the street that's sending a surge into your house. You have to ask why and ask again.

Keep asking until you get to the cause:

Why is the light going out?

Why is the ballast bad?

Why is the circuit breaker breaking?

Why is the transformer on the street surging?

The root cause isn't the light bulb going out. It is somewhere down the road, and usually you have to ask a lot of questions to get there.

A leader has to understand the person they're talking to. The questions help you position yourself to understand what's going on and why it's going on. Hopefully, as you discover things through that process, not only are *you* discovering the solution to the problem, but the person who's sitting with you, the one you're asking questions of, is also discovering the solutions to their problem through that process.

It's not so much that you have the answer. You are helping them discover for themselves as you ask great questions.

Conversely, what happens when you say, "I'll just tell you what to do and you go do it"?

That leaves you both kind of stuck.

Moving Out of Your Comfort Zone and Into Someone Else's

Be conscious of how to help the person you're communicating with to be the most comfortable. Be willing to move into someone else's arena or comfort zone.

What do I mean by that?

You want the person you're talking with to feel at ease. So if the person works on the floor, chances are they will feel much more comfortable talking to you on the floor than being called to your office.

Move out of your land and into theirs, out on the production line, or in a warehouse, or wherever. Physically move to their location.

Next, do your best to understand the person and what their situation is.

Where are they coming from culturally, educationally?

Perhaps according to their culture, communicating with someone over a meal is much more effective than communicating with them in a conference room.

You can communicate much better when you are aware of someone's:

- Condition
- Situation
- Concerns
- Needs

They will feel more comfortable. They'll be more willing to share.

Consciously try adjusting yourself rather than requiring them to adjust. You'll be pleasantly surprised by your impact if you operate from this perspective.

I was asked to go run an operation in New Jersey. Upon arriving, I felt lots of tension. Lots of union issues were unresolved. There were many, many conflicts between the company and the team that was working inside the operation.

To make a long story short, my decision was to try to find four to five leaders in the operation that I could start communicating with out on the floor on a daily basis.

What were the issues?

What was going on with them?

Why was this such a horrible condition?

Over a series of months, I was able to develop a relationship with four shop stewards sufficient enough to build some trust. Within about a year and a half, the whole organization came full circle to be top in safety and climbing the ladder in performance. They decided to decertify the union and remove it from the organization.

I think the change came about because I had cared about the team.

The company then followed our team's lead to care enough to say, "We're here. We support you. We will do what we can to have a great relationship, work through these issues, fix problems, and resolve the conflicts that we've had."

I don't think the organization that I was working with had ever seen the de-certification of a union in its thirty- or forty-year history. It's still that way today. The organization is still running fairly well.

I learned a lot of lessons about how to make those things stick. In the first organization that I took over to run on my own, I made wonderful performance improvements with the team that I was there with, but they didn't stick; the company fell apart within two years.

Ninety percent of the work with that team in New Jersey was done in their operation somewhere, either in a small room or out on the floor. It was done in areas where the team felt most comfortable.

That's how you're going to be able to hear from the team. They're going to be more authentic and honest with you, because they're comfortable. Most of my time with the team was spent in their parts of the operation, not in my office or not in a conference room somewhere.

Taking Notes, Using Body Language, and Giving Feedback

You need to show interest — honest, authentic interest — in the person you're communicating with.

When someone sees you taking notes, they see you are trying:

- To listen
- To understand
- To comprehend
- To remember

Taking notes allows you to return to key points and to reiterate a point to the individual. They understand that you're trying hard to understand what they are saying. Taking notes reassures people that you will remember what's important, versus just trying to listen and retain every word.

There is probably some connection between taking notes and body language. They run together. Taking notes forces you to use good body language while you are communicating with someone. Be aware of note taking and body language and try to use them while in conversation.

Body language is nonverbally communicating the idea that you're wide open.

How do you show with your body that you are listening?

Early on in my career, I made big mistakes:

- I folded my arms in meetings.

- I turned my shoulder to someone who was communicating.

- I did things with my body that communicated a lack of attention or care.

I later learned:

- To lean my body toward someone who was speaking to me

- To keep my arms uncrossed

- To maintain good eye contact

These are all little things that we have a tendency to take for granted. They are really necessary for good communication.

Feedback is your ability to say back to someone what they are communicating to you.

Feedback allows you to establish that:

- You hear what the person is saying.
- You are on the same level.
- You have the same understanding.

Many times, when I say, "What I think I hear you saying is..." the other person says, "No, that's not what I'm saying at all."

You're trying to ensure that what you think you're hearing is what the other person is saying.

When you reflect back to someone, "What I believe I'm hearing you say is..." then that gives them the opportunity to affirm yes, you're on the right track; or no, they're trying to communicate something else and what you're hearing is not what they're trying to say.

Many times, you might think you're on the same page with someone but you're just not. When they articulate something and you run it through your own translating or filtering system, the way you interpret those words is not what the person is trying to express to you.

Feeding the words back to the individual always helps bring clarity to a conversation. You don't need to say the words exactly the way they said them to you — that's not the point. The point is to try to get the essence of what they're trying to communicate. I'm always surprised by how many times I can correct misunderstandings by doing this.

KNOW YOURSELF WELL

When you are in a leadership role, or managing an organization or people, one of the best things you can do for that team is to know yourself well. Do not be afraid of an assessment.

There are multiple kinds of assessments. When I first was exposed to these, I had a bit of trepidation. I was fairly nervous.

I wondered:

What are they going to find out about me?

Maybe I have some kind of weird thing going on inside of me.

The truth is that assessment gave me great insight. Embrace anything that can give you a 360-degree view of yourself. Ask for them. Don't be afraid of them.

Assessments can help you:

- Become way more self-aware
- Communicate better
- Understand your strengths and weaknesses
- Understand where you need help
- Understand why you might struggle in communication

Assessments are really critical. If you assume everything is fine or that you're the greatest communicator ever, you miss out on learning how you can improve.

Understanding Who You Are and How You're Wired

Unless you're trying to educate yourself, you can get stuck.

Strive to:

- Educate yourself

- Understand yourself
- Have an awareness of yourself

You can really open your mind by learning in different ways. Read and digest more information from other people who have experienced things in ways that are really different from how you have experienced them. Learn about other people.

Find out about other people's:

- Personalities
- Discoveries
- Insights into other topics and situations

You can get a better understanding of where you are in positioning and in relation to these folks. You may find that compared to another person (or their understanding), your knowledge is limited or you might find it's fantastic.

Earlier in my life, I never really had the kind of education that I wanted. Through the years, I received tons and tons of great education, but I've never graduated with a master's degree, for instance.

I've had plenty of people working for me who have had doctorate degrees.

Some were very frustrated and would come to me and say, "I'm two levels below you in this work, and I'm very upset and frustrated. I have a degree and you don't. Why is it that you're in that position and I'm stuck here in this position?"

When they posed the question to me, they would tell me things like, "I got my degree in 1992. That's when I completed my master's, so I should be moving up by now."

But twenty years later, they hadn't done anything to educate themselves past their initial degree. They believed that once they'd finished some level of understanding or education, they were done. They hadn't stayed on top of their education; they hadn't tried to discover new things. They were stuck.

When you stop learning, your ability to influence and impact people and situations around you is very limited. It inhibits your ability to lead at higher levels. Staying at the top level is all about education—not necessarily formal education—but education: bringing self-awareness to a higher level.

How many hours in a day or a week do you focus on seeking to understand and educate yourself about who you are and how you're wired?

Try quantifying your pursuit of real self-awareness in real time. If you're not measuring it, you're not going to do it.

Are you going to try to read twelve books this year?

What are their topics going to be?

Try to quantify your self-education however you would like, with a number or a process, so that you can hold yourself accountable to the goal.

Open to Feedback and Find the Right Kind of Mentor

Being open to feedback means that you're posturing yourself so that you can hear even the hard words delivered to you. Sometimes words are going to be not harsh, but hard. It may be feedback that you aren't living up to a level or understanding that you think you are, or that you aren't necessarily performing at the level that you should be.

If you can posture yourself to hear those words, that's fantastic. When you have good relationships with folks and trust them, and they trust you, the feedback they give doesn't feel weird, icky, or strange. It's an honest and honorable kind of conversation in which they say what they think you really need to work on and why.

When you build those relationships, eventually you find a mentor.

A mentor is someone who will:

- Pour into you

- Click with you
- Teach you
- Be someone you want to listen to
- Help you adjust
- Stretch you

A mentor is not going to accept nonsense from you or let you sit in a little pity party, or let you be a victim of a condition. That's tough, because a lot of folks want to hear the words that tickle their ears.

The mentor aspect is critical. The problem is, a lot of organizations try to legislate mentorship — requiring that people have a mentor or become a mentor. There's more to mentoring than can be legislated, however.

The relationship between mentor and mentee is something special. Maybe there's a spiritual aspect of their life that you share.

When you meet someone, you may think: *This person's really focused and connected.*

Maybe you feel good around this person because you know or have heard about the experiences that they've had and they're not all easy, but the person still seems to have joy in their life, and they're continuing to walk through life in a positive way. You're looking for mentors who are going to stretch you and add value to your way of working; they're not going to allow you to hold on to the idea that you're a victim of a condition, for instance.

Understanding Your Strengths and How Others See You

I love the StrengthsFinder software by Gallup. I think that it does a wonderful job. You answer a number of questions and it shows you your five key strengths. Then it gives you good words, and good word pictures, to help you understand how the strengths show up in your work and your life.

Knowing your strengths, however you find them, is very important.

Through the Window

We don't all see everything the same way. There's the idea as you and I communicate, it's like we're looking through a window that's between us.

You're projecting something and you're hoping that I see that same projection through the window.

The projection might be about a certain:

- Person
- Personality
- Communication style
- Idea

You're projecting it through the window and hoping that I pick it up just the way you're seeing it. The reality is that I'm looking through the window, looking at you, and seeing something totally different from what you're projecting.

How can you understand that?

How can you start to dig into the difference between what people are seeing versus what you are trying to project?

I don't know that I have the answer for how you go about doing that, because everyone is wired so differently.

In order to find the answer, you have to use your strengths and understand your weaknesses. You want to get very good at projecting an honest, clear view of yourself, because that's what people are going to pick up. They're going to see things about you that you probably don't even recognize you're projecting.

You want to be aware of this in your communications.

Remember when you're projecting something through your window to ask yourself:

When they look in, do they see the same thing I'm projecting or something different?

How do I give them the freedom to tell me what I'm saying and what they're seeing are two different things?

Going back to the idea that you can accomplish more when people are comfortable is key. You want the lines of communication to be open enough so that if something isn't working or isn't clear, the other person can speak up.

How are you positioning yourself?

When you understand your strengths and the strengths of the team you're working with you can quickly see what piece of the picture is missing.

Let's say we're working on a project and we need ten different skill sets. You know going in that your current team only has five, and the odds of finding one person who single-handedly has all remaining five skills are pretty slim. When you know the strengths of your team, you can see which blank spots need to be filled. You can assemble a team of people who have a good mix of strengths.

Now you really have a shot at doing something very, very good. You're not stuck with only three people and big holes in your skill sets.

You want to find out who is on your team. Not just their strengths, but how they're wired, how they come to the table, all those kinds of things. When you assess your team, you want to know your team members and what they can bring.

One of the mistakes that people make is not understanding that they need a lot of diversity and lots of different skill sets. If they don't know what a particular person's strengths are, then the odds of being able to use that person on their team to make the company better are slim to none.

You'll discover that as you come to know yourself better, you'll feel healthier. It's not a show. You're not trying to be something that you're not. You're not trying to force things.

Knowing your strengths is a natural, more normal way of living. It's a God-gifted way of living. God put these talents and strengths in you.

You will be happier and healthier when you can:

- Get in touch with your strengths.
- Work with them.
- Take the time to know who you are.

KEEP YOUR HANDS AND YOUR MIND WIDE OPEN

Earlier in my management and leadership life, it was very difficult for me to keep myself open to possibilities. I was trying to control and command whatever situation was given to me. I wasn't necessarily open to anyone or anything else. I felt I had to do and control everything.

I later learned that it was really about impact and influence.

Seeking First to Understand

It's very easy to think: *I want you to understand me before I try to understand you.*

But I think that's backwards.

A popular Christian prayer often attributed to St. Francis entreats:

Oh divine Master, grant that I may not so much seek...

To be understood as to understand....

I think it's better to take a minute, to take a breath, and even to say your own prayer:

Lord, please help me to understand this person, situation, or condition.

Make a conscious effort to really hear what the other person is trying to tell you before you run to answers and solutions, or even to ask questions. It may feel like a difficult thing to do. It felt difficult for me at first.

Empty Yourself So You Can Receive

Typically in business or in life, you're running from one situation to the next situation. It's life; it's just how it goes.

What do you do that will allow you to take a minute, or a breath?

How will you let go of whatever it is that you were just in the middle of so that you can move to the next conversation, or group of people, or situation?

As a leader, that's required of you all day long! You're running from meeting to meeting, condition to condition, situation to situation.

At what point between those times are you taking a few minutes to really empty your mind and your body?

How do you go about doing that?

I think it would be different for you than it would be for me, but do I even take the time?

Do I allow myself the time to take the long way around to the next conversation so that I can breathe for a second, release some of the tension or release some of the critical nature of that past conversation so that I can move to the next conversation?

Or is it just that I go to the next one and I'm carrying all of that into the room with me, and I can't hear anything that's happening in the next conversation?

On an hour-by-hour basis, you want to start your day with this idea of some contemplative time in prayer or meditation. Prayer may not be the way you've thought about it. I grew up thinking that prayer was kind of me, speaking to God, and telling Him about all my conditions and situations.

As I grow older, that conversation is more like me asking myself:

When am I listening?

When am I just emptying my mind?

When am I emptying my heart and allowing God to speak to me versus me speaking to Him?

Now I want to ask these questions daily, weekly, monthly, in a bigger way than I ever did when I was younger.

I'm discovering that that leads to a much more rich experience than telling God what I need or want.

It's much better than me directing God, "Hey God, I need this. I need that. I've got to work on this. You've got to work on that. I need help with this. I need help with that."

I've learned to give God space, and to give my heart and mind space, for the next situation, condition, or conversation.

Repeating Back What You Heard

It's important to use words and phrases that reassure the person who's trying to communicate to you that:

- You are listening to them.
- You understand what they are saying.
- You are tracking with them.

Use questions such as:

This is what I'm hearing; am I hearing you correctly?

This is what I'm understanding; am I understanding you correctly?

This is what I think you're trying to convey to me; am I on the right track?

Don't use a coarse, "Yeah, yeah, yeah. I understand. Let's go."

Try to find the right phrases and feedback so the person understands you are working hard to really digest what they're trying to explain to you.

Steer away from flippant comments like, "I understand; let's move on to the next thing. I gotcha."

Indicating that you care and are listening is simple, really, but it's a lot bigger than we might understand or give credit to. We get so busy it's hard to remember this. Rushing through the other person's explanation kills the relationship. It reduces your ability to build relationships.

In every conversation and every phase with the team of people that you're working with, you have the opportunity to build:

- Trust
- Respect
- Honor
- Integrity

Receive, Rather Than Give Information

As a leader or a manager, there's a perception that you should have the answers.

You're the one.

You're the Answer Man or the Answer Woman.

Really, that's not the posture that's going to get the team, the organization, or you, to where you are trying to go. It's just *not* going to happen.

Instead, you want to position yourself to open up so you can hear and understand. Position yourself so you can discover *with* your team the best path to take. Don't try to be the Answer Man or Woman. Discover the answers and the way forward with your organization, and let people know you are invested in creating the path together.

Again, promote conversations of questions more than ones in which you're giving the answers.

If you have the answers, you don't necessarily need to give them. Sometimes as the leader, you're mentoring and coaching other team members, helping them to discover the answer, versus giving them the answer. This is a better way forward for you and for them.

Sometimes, you might feel impatient or like you have to rush.

You tell people, "Well, just do this, and this, and this."

If you work in this way, you might leave a lot of potential benefits behind, because you're just doing it the way you know will be a quick fix, or trying quickly to move on to the next thing.

But maybe your answer isn't *the* answer. Maybe you need to ask the questions again, this time of the people you are working with.

As a leader, everyone wants you to give the answers, but the reality is that your answers aren't necessarily what they need. They may need help — to discover, to understand, to process — but they don't necessarily need you to give them the answers to their problems.

When you open up to receive other's answers and ideas, the possibilities are endless. Considering the possibilities doesn't mean that you're not satisfied with the current situations or the current products. It just means that you're open to the idea that maybe there's a better result to be created or found.

Look at Toyota. They didn't kill the Corolla when they built the Prius. They just kept dreaming of bigger and better possibilities. The Prius is a great car, but it's a different concept; it's a different idea than a Corolla.

Don't stop dreaming. Don't be satisfied that you have the product you want. There are just so many other possibilities. It's worth trying to perfect what you already have, but remember to stay open to the possibilities. Don't limit your ability to dream. That's a mistake.

CHAPTER
TWO

Educating Everyone in the Organization

ASSESS THE POSITION OF THE PEOPLE YOU'RE TRYING TO EDUCATE

A lot of organizations use a cookie-cutter approach to training teams and staff.

Someone will bring a curriculum and say, "This is the best way to educate your team."

Unfortunately, they don't know your team; they haven't assessed your team. They have come up with what probably is a really good educational tool; however, for any number of reasons, it's just not going to work.

Then you're left wondering:

Why doesn't this seem to stick?

I spent all this money. It didn't seem to help the organization or the team in any way.

Care Enough to Know the Team

I think that when most leaders come to the table they are already very busy. They have a million things to do, a million things to work on. It's easy to get isolated and insulated in an organization. It's easy to get disconnected from the staff. This disconnected state affects the whole team, not just you.

You have to create the time and space in which you're having lots of conversations with staff. Get close enough so that they feel comfortable and a feeling of trust develops. Make sure that in a conversation, meeting, or in any other kind of activity that you're conducting in your organization, people feel a natural indication or inclination to talk with you.

It takes time.

Most leaders struggle with having enough time, so prioritize your time and be intentional about it. Take the time to meet and greet the folks who are in an operation, in the office, and doing the day-to-day work.

Talk to staff. You will get to know them, but at the same time, talk to your leadership team about how to create the kinds of activities that are going to allow you to really get to mingle and spend time with the staff.

That can be done in many ways, and a lot of them can be fun. Allow for these activities and understand that they are a part of the education process. Make the time for group activities like:

- Once-a-month birthday celebrations

- Quarterly dessert socials

- Ten or fifteen minutes at the end of the day to allow people to build their knowledge of one another

- End of the day time to share dessert, drink coffee, and get to know folks

- Organizing games after work

These are all part of the education and the getting-to-know-you processes.

You may be in a different place in your life than your team is. As a leader you gain some success, knowledge, and insight. Sometimes visiting with staff can feel as if you're going backwards, because you're spending time with people who maybe don't know everything that you know, or people who you perceive don't understand things the way you understand.

It's critical that you understand that you can learn a ton from them, and they can learn a ton from you, if you just take the time.

Tell Stories About Your Own Life

Many leaders want to tell stories. Sometimes the tendency is to tell stories of self-righteous kinds of behaviors.

They may be intended to show:

- How big and strong they are
- How effective they are
- How intelligent they are
- What prowess (intellectual or otherwise) they have
- How wise they are

Leaders who tell these stories feel like everyone needs to know how good they are. This is backwards. People can relate a lot better to a leader who is self-aware.

They need to hear from you that:

- You're human
- You've made tons of mistakes
- You have learned from your mistakes
- You've grown and developed as a result

A good leader relates through stories. Not all stories have to be negative, actually; I don't mean you should degrade yourself. But don't be afraid to share where you have failed, learned from it, and grown from it. You can show through your stories that making mistakes can lead to education, improved understanding, and help you to jump higher or do better going forward.

Many times in my career, I've told a story in which I couldn't accomplish something or it wasn't going the way that I wanted it to go. I've been able to explain how I was able to maneuver or learn some things that allowed me to do it better the next time.

One example I use is when I took over my first operation in Boston, Massachusetts. I was the leader of the whole operation and was very successful with the team there. We did a lot of great things. We implemented new procedures. We started a process that the organization adapted throughout the whole United States; it was a wonderful experience. I was asked to take over an area within New York, and leave the Boston group.

Within about a year to year and a half, everything that I had done in Boston fell apart. When I reflected on my time there, I realized that things fell apart because the changes we made there were based on my own personality, my own charisma. It was all about me, my influencing everything with my own personality.

When I went to New York, I did a lot of the same things. But I built a team of high-capacity people around me. I allowed the staff and all parts of the organization to create the changes instead of just me doing it. From that day to this, the New York operation continues to thrive and go forward.

It wasn't about me in New York. It was more about putting systems, processes, and people in place, and allowing *every* level of the organization, not just Ron Nottingham, to engage in the process of improvement.

Gratitude, Humility, and Curiosity Open Communication

First and foremost as a leader, you need to truly be thankful. Nothing, but nothing, is going to happen in your organization without people. If you think it is all you, you are just fooling yourself.

You must have gratitude toward the customer and toward the people who are making these things happen within your organization. Being appreciative and really respectful of their work is very important.

Self-awareness can really promote humility. I own a small service repair center in California; it has probably ten to fifteen people working in it. There's not a job in that organization—other than marketing and managing overall leadership management of that organization—that I can do. These folks repair motor homes, cars, trucks, and buses. They do all kinds of stuff technically; they do all kinds of custom welding.

It's a kind of technical work that I don't have a clue about.

As a leader, you cannot possibly be gifted enough to know everything about every aspect of an operation or organization. You need to be humble and have enough humility to understand there are a lot of other gifted people there as well. Maybe their skill sets are not going to allow them to lead the overall organization, or their talent mix isn't going to give them the ability to manage the whole organization, but the reality is that they're doing things that you are never going to be able to do!

Be grateful and humble to people with different kinds of talents. Be grateful to those who really make your organization run and move successfully.

Be careful that you're not allowing their position to affect you in a positive or negative way.

What do I mean by that?

It may be easy to think that a leader is the most important position in an organization.

That's just untrue.

It is a very important position, but if you don't have great technical skills in a technical organization, or engineering skills in an engineering organization, you're not going to be successful, no matter how great you can be. As the leader, you just can't lose sight of that.

When you take the time to be inquisitive about what people in the organization do and how they do it, it shows a level of respect and honor for them. Their jobs in the organization are much different than yours, and their jobs are just as important.

In an organization I worked with, the CEO had six hundred people working for him in a production environment. When he came in as the new CEO of that organization, he spent time with *every* team member in the organization. It was only ten or fifteen minutes per person, but he watched them do their work and asked them questions. It made all the difference for his run as the CEO of that organization.

Really try to understand where the people are. You truly need understanding to lead successfully. That understanding can result from assessment that either you or a professional firm conduct with intentionality and clear quantification. Make sure that you assess as you move forward.

BUILD APPROPRIATE CURRICULUM

Another important benefit of assessment is that it helps

you know where your team is, and therefore, what kind of training will be most effective. If you're not assessing where your team is when it comes to education, it's just going to be a swing and a miss. It's going to be frustrating. The people will be frustrated, you will be frustrated as a leader, and you'll wonder why they just don't get it.

I have seen this over and over in organizations. They'll tell me that they have given their teams training and coaching and it just didn't stick, so it's not worth the energy.

One reason training doesn't stick is because there's no assessment to find where the teams are and what's really going to stick at that moment. In a nutshell, it's really up to the leader to understand that. It's not up to the team member to try to get that aligned and figured out.

Another reason training doesn't work is because people need repeated experiences to remember and apply what they learn. You have to train your team multiple times in order for the training to stick.

Understand the Average Educational Background of the Team

Much of the training material and processes that are used by organizations are developed by engineers and trainers who have great educations. They have doctorate degrees and formal education. But if the average education of the team that you're working with is at a high school level, then your training must also be on that level. I'm not knocking high school education; the point is that you've got to start them where they are, and that's high school.

If the material doesn't match their last level of education, they're probably not going to be able to grasp what you're trying to teach. In fact, I would say if they haven't been in school or a training environment within the last fifteen years, you may want to back up to a tenth- or ninth-grade level of education when you're assembling the training.

Understand the Family Background of the Team

I think family dynamics play a role in how people learn.

What do I mean by that?

Sometimes, depending on the families and cultures, males get treated one way and females get treated another way. You need to understand that family dynamic.

In some cultures there's a really high level of respect for elders in a family. The senior population is treated at the highest levels of respect and their knowledge is treated as treasure.

In some cultures, like here in the United States, there's little respect for elders in a family. We cast our elders out when they get old because we don't want to deal with them.

You have to have at least some basic understanding of what's happening within that family and what's happening within that culture. It can be hard to know a lot about the people in your teams; that's why as I said in the beginning of this book, you have to spend the time to get to know people. It takes time for them to open up about what's happening within their home and what's happening within their family.

I'm not recommending that you pry into their personal lives, but I recommend that you spend enough time that you get to get to know them, and they have the opportunity to share personal things.

Why is that important?

In one organization that I work with, the staff is made up of mostly women. As I got to know these women, I learned that many of them have three or four children. They come out of families who expect that they'll have dinner on the table every night by the time their husbands come home. Team members might hardly have a minute to think about brushing their teeth at night, let alone spending time on whatever homework there might be from a training at work.

If you knew this about your team, you could take into account that their time is very limited outside of the workplace. If you know that going in, then you have a chance of being fairly successful with training. If you don't know that going in, and you're giving them things to read after they leave the office that day, it won't go very well. So take that into consideration when you're designing the training.

Understand the Cultural Background of the Team

Cultures can shape many aspects of life for people, such as their ability:

- To learn
- To comprehend
- To move

You need to consider the cultural background in order to be as successful at training as you want to be.

Throughout the United States, there are pockets of different ethnicities. Those cultures bring certain kinds of styles of learning, doing, and being that impact a person's ability to grasp and to comprehend. If you're not paying attention to them, your training's going to miss.

For instance, an example could be that I've taken this training that was produced by X-Y-Z company. It's designed for a U.S. company that has American workers.

Then I want to train a group in a California company using the same curriculum, but the California company has a high quotient of Vietnamese workers. Their cultural background is going to affect their ability to digest and apply that information. You have to be aware of that.

It all goes back to the essential assessment questions:

- Where are they coming from?
- Where are they now?

So many times we swing and miss because we're delivering a training or some kind of education without considering:

- Who are these people?
- Where have they come from?
- How have they been educated in the past?

Understand the Current Life Conditions of the Team

Life circumstances and conditions affect a person's

ability to learn and to take in new information. You want to be keenly aware of any of the factors in the lives of team members that enhance or injure their ability to learn.

When you take life conditions into consideration as you're trying to mentor, coach, or train groups, you're going to be much more successful than if you just decide flippantly that these folks need a certain kind of training.

Life conditions can range from caring for elderly parents to simply having lots of conflict in the home. Maybe the training has to go a little slower than you might want.

Or it could be that life conditions are really good for the team that you're working with and they're in a season of life in which everything is beautiful. In that case, maybe you are going too slowly with your training and they are getting bored. Maybe you decide they're ready for more new curriculum to work through.

It's important for you to know what's going on, positively and negatively, if you can.

Usually when someone tells me, "I don't know what's really happening with my team," that tells me that they're not focused — you're probably not working hard enough to understand who they are and what they're up against.

When I talk about what's happening in life, I mean what's happening at home *and* what's happening in the organization. I mean what's happening in your business or in your company as well, whatever affects the members of the team.

An organization could be wildly successful, and that would have a positive impact on development. Or the company could be in a time of struggling or not performing or producing the way that is desired. That's most likely going to have a negative impact on how people can learn, grow, and develop.

When you're designing or choosing your training, experiment. You may need to test some training, or test some way of educating your team, before you roll out something that's bigger.

What do I mean by that?

Conduct tests on new projects, on new information, and on ways of educating or working through a problem. You don't want to roll out something as the latest and greatest tool only to have it die six months later because you didn't try it out first. As the leader you need to be prepared to recognize when something isn't working and change plans if necessary.

It's better to try it out first and make any changes before you take it to the staff. I like to use the word *countermeasures.* If you find something doesn't work, you try something different. And if that doesn't work, move on to the next countermeasure.

You don't turn it into a legacy or a monument of what we're going to do from now on and forever, because the odds are that you're going to have to make an adjustment.

MAKE IT FUN, AND THAT WILL MAKE IT STICK

When I'm talking about training or curricula in these settings, they should *not* be like the education you see in school. You may think I'm suggesting a curriculum based on books, but that's really not what I'm talking about.

I started at Toyota when I was nineteen years old, and everything that I learned that was fun stuck. Everything that was tied to stories had huge impacts on me as a person, because I could remember them.

Any time fun was attached to learning, it caught me by surprise and I enjoyed it. Previously I thought trainings would be dull and boring. I didn't even like using the word *training* as I began coaching and mentoring people. I thought it didn't indicate that we were going to have fun, laugh, and tell stories.

At that time the president at Toyota was Jim Press. He

was one of two people there who trained by telling personal stories.

Their stories were about:

- Life
- Customers
- Conditions

The stories always referred back to who we were as a team and what we were trying to accomplish with our customers.

Then a Vice President, Dave Sloan, would do the same thing. Sometimes he would tell the story through poetry.

In our meetings, he would tell:

- Personal stories
- Life stories
- Historical stories about work and people

His stories were always tied to a training or to some kind of information that stayed with me.

At the end of the session I'd think: *Wow! That was really impactful. That was important; I need to remember that.*

And I could remember it because I could remember the story. Fun and stories are tied together; keep that first and foremost in your brain.

Making It Easy

To make it easy for you and your trainees, work to get to know:

- Where people are in the process
- What's happening with them in your organization
- What's happening with them in their lives
- What's happening within their culture
- What's happening within their home

Once you know the people better, you can address finding an easy way to teach these folks.

What's an easy way to present information?

How do you want to share what you're trying to do?

How do you want them to process?

It becomes easy because you have put in the effort to "seek first to understand and then to be understood."

I can't tell you what will be the easiest way for your circumstances. Making it easy will all depend on all of the findings that you've discovered along the way. You will find what's easy because of all of your hard work to make sure that you know your staff. That will tell you what's going to be palatable and natural for learning.

You want the material to be easy for them to learn and to grasp, and to use this information in the organization to become better at what they do.

Keeping It Light

Most of the organizations that I work with are not up against life-or-death situations. I usually don't work with doctors; I usually don't work with people who will encounter a major crisis if this training goes wrong or doesn't work out the way I want.

Keeping it light means that it's okay:

- To have fun
- To make mistakes
- To try new things
- To be yourself
- To let them be themselves

In most situations, there's not going to be any horrible condition if the training goes wrong for a minute or it doesn't work out exactly the way you wanted it to. Don't be too serious.

I'm not saying not to be serious about teaching and coaching people, but don't be so serious that you think you're the professor or a disciplinarian. Remember the things that you didn't like in the teachers that you had through life. You're not in that arena, so don't worry or think like that.

Keep the training — this understanding, this coaching — light and easy.

When you feel the tension in the room of people stressing over whether they're understanding the material, adjust what's happening in the discussion. Tell a joke.

Lighten the mood by:

- Telling a joke
- Telling a story
- Taking a break

Feel free to say, "It's not life or death, let's just take a minute and process. We don't have to stress out over this."

Telling Personal Stories

There are many reasons to use storytelling as a part of your training.

Stories help:

- To make you real and human
- To make things stick

- To make people understand that you are no better or worse than they are

Using stories in trainings helps to show that you, like your trainees, are coming through life; you're dealing with life issues just like they are. It's true that you have a different role to play in the organization and that you may know some things that will help them become better at their craft, but your stories can show that you are no more important than the staff. What you share can help them be better and more productive at what they do.

I can recall stories from trainings I attended thirty years ago. They still make me pause and think: *That still sticks in my brain!*

These stories are really important. The personal stories drive home the effectiveness of what it is that you might be teaching. They drive home how things work.

One story I tell is about a project in which we were going to change the transportation system for a whole metropolitan area. It was all going well until September came. Then suddenly the whole thing fell apart. We wondered what the heck was going on.

We finally realized that we hadn't taken back-to-school traffic into account. In September, school buses got back on the road, parents got back on the road with their kids, and it messed everything up. We had to re-work the whole thing!

Those people retold that story three or four times in other parts of the organization I was working with. As people were revamping their transportation systems, that's the story that rumbled through. It was telling and retelling those little stories about what went right and what went wrong that helped the initiative to move quickly and become successful.

The meat and potatoes was how we were going about setting up the transportation schedules, but the reality is, the stories helped people:

- Move
- Have fun
- Laugh—or cry—about how badly we screw up

It was the stories that really helped people grasp and comprehend what we were trying to do, the effect that we were having, and the difference we were making within the organization.

The stories you tell can be about business, but they can also be about you personally or a story you've heard about other folks.

I have grown tremendously through the bits and pieces of people's lives they have shared with me. I was once working with a coach, telling him how broken I was in my work and what was happening with me.

He was able to stop me and say, "Listen, let me tell you a personal story about my life, and how broken I was."

He was much more superior in the organization than I was, and when he was a young person he had been much more broken than me! That story had a *huge* impact on me.

It made me realize that:

- I was not alone.

- I was not the only guy who's made tremendous mistakes.

- I could still potentially right some of those wrongs and be successful.

So many personal stories of that kind have had a huge impact on my life. The stories helped me see things differently. You just can't put a price tag on that form of training and coaching.

Breaking the Ice

Even though some may be weirded out by icebreakers or fun activities before the training gets started, they are usually some of the best parts of the training.

Don't skip this step. Put some energy into figuring out what would be a good way to help people:

- Break the ice
- Get to know each other
- Start off on the right foot

That piece of the training process is much bigger than most folks give credit. Be intentional.

Really try to figure out:

What would add a lot of value in the start-off?

Don't make that the last thing that you think about before you get into the room. It will hurt you.

It Takes More Than Once

Training has to be repeatable. You have to keep doing it. So many organizations wonder why associates don't understand or remember the training a month, a year, two years later.

Why don't the trainees remember?

Think about a local church. A thriving local church will train people every Sunday morning. They do worship; they do a message; they're basically opening the Bible and educating the congregation every single Sunday. They — and God — are hoping and praying that people will come to church every week and get the message.

Then there's the expectation that there will be other activities in addition to that once-a-week training. Maybe you're in a small group of shared interests or for support; that's like the coaching you might get at work. Then there's an expectation that you may go to some social event, which is like the times at work set aside for people to get to know one another better.

Everything around the church is set up so that you're constantly involved in:

- Training
- Coaching
- Edifying
- Building each other up

Churches that are thriving do these things very well.

You need to do the same thing for your organization. You can't just expect that you will train people and then never return to that topic for a year.

It's unfair and unrealistic to have that expectation. You can do so much better when you invest the time and money to educate your teams at every level, consistently and purposefully.

CHAPTER

THREE

Leadership and Self-Awareness

LIFELONG LEARNING IS CRITICAL

As a young boy in the education system, I really believed that I couldn't learn. I dropped out of school in the tenth grade. I felt like there was no way; no matter how I was wired, I could not learn.

When I was nineteen years old I proposed to my future wife. She said she would, but only on the condition that I return to school, so I did.

I met a woman who helped me with English to prepare me for the GED. She helped me to understand that I just learned differently. I grew to understand that I *could* learn, and in fact everyone can learn. It is a matter of just discovering *how* you learn.

From that point to this one it's been a lifelong journey of never stopping.

There are so many things that help you:

- Grow
- Develop
- See the world differently
- Deepen your understanding

You have to take the time to relate, to learn, and to develop yourself.

Learning New Things Every Month

I spent a lot of years at Toyota, and one of the things that I was trained to do is develop a good annual plan. That plan includes setting monthly goals, including educational goals.

Write it down—not in Excel spreadsheets, but using a pencil and paper.

Over the course of twelve months, how many things are you're going to read?

What are the subjects that you want to read about?

What do you want to learn about?

Then systematically, every single month:

- Track your progress.
- Find the right material.
- Find the things that you're interested in

It can be anything: things that are critical to your life,

like investing in your retirement, or a special interest, like learning about flowers. The idea is that you want to posture yourself to become a lifelong learner.

To be successful in your learning goals, just as with many other goals in this book, you want to measure and evaluate them. If you don't measure them and evaluate whether you're accomplishing what you're trying to do, you're not going to be as successful.

Put things into some kind quantitative measurement: number of books, for instance. Breaking them down seems to help me be successful, and it may help you.

Seek Best Practices in Your Sphere

Like most people, you may have a tendency to believe that where you are today is a pretty good place. Then you might get complacent, and change becomes a little more difficult.

The Marines have a saying: "While someone is thinking about it, someone else is doing it."

You want to be someone who gets it done. Try to get out of your comfort zone and look for things to learn.

I've been involved in helping a few churches in my career. Once I was in Texas visiting family members. I sought three or four churches there that I thought could add some value for some of the churches that

I'm trying to help. I tried to see their best practices.

What are they doing with guest services?

What are they doing with volunteers?

How are they loving on the community and trying to fulfill the needs of the community?

Look for best practices always, wherever you are.

Toyota was great at this. They consistently sent us out to find best practices inside and outside of our own organization. Do that in life; do that in work. You can do that in whatever context you want.

Seek best practices and people who are just doing it a little bit better, a little bit differently from you. That adds value for you, your organization, your team, and your family. It's just a wonderful way to continue to grow and educate yourself.

You can also learn from everyone else's mistakes. Learn from other folks and the mistakes that they make. Then you don't need to make them yourself.

When you see best practices, these people are not showing you the ten things they did wrong. They're showing you the one thing they did well, and it's going well for them. That's what you want to see.

Finding Good Mentors

My experience with mentorship is that sometimes companies try to facilitate or implement a mentoring program. Some of those probably work. But in both becoming a mentor and having good mentors, I have found that it works out best if the mentee seeks the mentor.

So when I'm looking for someone to help me with a particular problem or issue that I'm fighting through, I'm looking for that man or woman who has been there, done that, and come out the other side and is better off for it.

That means I have to be looking for them, and they're not looking for me necessarily. The idea is to try to pick your head up, and to understand that a lot of these folks who have gone before you can give you guidance and coaching.

My wife and I read *The Love Dare* in a small book group. It was a great book and we had a lot of fun reading it. Most of the couples in our group had been married twenty-five years or so. At the end of the book, there was a reference to a couple who had been married fifty years.

Our book group found a couple in our church who had been married fifty years. We asked them to come and mentor us, and they did.

We wanted to ask them:

- What's important at fifty years versus twenty-five years?

- What at twenty-five years did you think was important, that just wasn't?

- We wanted them to give us their insight and their wisdom.

What they told us was absolutely amazing. But we had to make it happen by doing the work of connecting with them. This experience didn't happen without effort.

We had to:

- Invite them
- Buy their dinner
- Spend time with them
- Figure out what kind of questions we wanted to ask

They didn't come looking for us; we went looking for them. The relationship turned out to be a great thing.

So that's an example of finding mentors at this stage of my life. When I was younger, I had a great mentor at Toyota named Dave Sloan. He took me under his wing when I was just a young guy of twenty-five trying to figure everything out.

Now I'm fifty-five, so do the math. He has mentored me for years; I still go see him once or twice a year for coaching and mentoring. He and his wife Betty are now lifelong friends of ours.

Finding the right mentor takes time. You're not necessarily going to connect with someone right out of the gate. It may take you four or five tries before you find that one person whose mentoring works well for both of you. Don't give up on the process. Seek good mentors.

John Maxwell, author of *The 21 Irrefutable Laws of Leadership*, talks about the "Law of the Lid," which states that you must continue to learn and grow and develop your leadership skills, or you become the limiting factor for your team. I believe this is true.

As the leader in your organization, family, or group, whoever's working with you stops where you stop. If you stop learning, if you stop trying to become a better person in whatever capacity, so will they. The team you are leading follows your example. If you don't keep learning, you can lose your team because in effect, you've put the lid on them.

I want to impress upon you as a leader that it is critical for you to constantly push yourself forward:

- Grow
- Look for new things
- Open your mind
- Look for what *could be* instead of settling for what is

LEADERS SHOW RESPECT, HONOR, AND DIGNITY TO EVERYONE

When you're a leader it's not easy:

- To show respect
- To be grace-filled
- To treat people honorably

The tendency is to want to push things forward. You may have a tendency to be more in control and command of things.

You may have a tendency to be abrupt because things have to get done:

- There are schedules.
- There are timelines.
- There are many demands on you.

It's easy to become like a dictator: "Just do what I'm telling you. Let's go, let's go, let's go!"

It's harder to be self-aware and conscious of what's

going on around you. Take a step back and take a breath. Realize that you're not any better than anyone else. You just have a different role there. Everyone puts their pants on one leg at a time. You can't be too full of yourself, even though being the leader is a tough role to play.

Your Role Is Different, Not Better

When you are in a leadership role, people have to listen to you. They have to give you a certain level of respect just because of your position and your power over them. That's potentially a problem. They have to behave that way toward you, but you don't have to give it back to them because you're the boss, the leader; you're in charge of it all.

Even though it may feel hard, it's really important to come to the table with the idea that you are the same.

Remind yourself that:

- You really do care about these people.
- They are just like you.
- They have families.
- They have many responsibilities in their lives.
- Their roles and responsibilities are much different than yours.

This is true whether they're manufacturing something,

working in a warehouse, or working in an office someplace where they're pushing paper.

The truth is that what they do is critical, and how you perceive it will have a huge impact on how you treat them and how you treat the things that are happening around them.

What you do as a leader is important, but even more important is to understand the intricate parts of the organization and what people around you are doing.

For instance, I think about the critical nature of the janitorial team.

Some people would say, "These are the folks who pick up the trash and clean up the place. We don't know their names; we don't know what's going on in their lives; we don't even take the time to say, 'Hello, how are you? What's going on with you?'"

In truth, if janitors don't do their job, our organization becomes a pigsty. Nobody wants to work in a place that nobody takes care of, that's trashy, dirty, and nasty. But sometimes leaders treat the staff taking care of that stuff as lesser than others. All they're doing is taking out the trash.

Janitors are an intricate part of the organization. If they don't do their job, the organization is probably going to be hurting in a few days. If you don't show up as a leader, in a few days, the organization will probably be okay.

So keep the right perspective on your role and responsibility, and make sure that as the leader, you honor everyone in the organization. They wouldn't be there if their role and responsibility wasn't critical to the job.

The Leader Is a Role Model

Sometimes it takes effort to be respectful and to show honor. You need to understand everyone's looking at you, so your posture is really important.

Take time in the morning:

- To get your head right
- To get alone with God
- To center yourself before you try to lead people

Everyone's watching you.

Imagine you come into work and your body language shows:

- You're grumpy.
- You look like you've had a rough night.
- Your mind is not in it.

People are looking. People are paying attention. How

you appear has an impact on the organization, unlike how other roles and responsibilities appear.

Be aware of what's going on with yourself. Constantly work to center yourself. The tide is going to rise and fall by how you behave. Sometimes leaders miss this point. They want to think that because they are human too, it's okay to get mad and frustrated. Maybe they vent their anger at people.

You must understand that as a leader, what you do is so much more hurtful or impactful for the group— positively or negatively—than what another team member does. Your behavior, and how you bring yourself to work every day, has a big impact on the organization.

Sometimes you have to work at showing a positive attitude. I'm not saying that you've got to come in and be the most extroverted, jumping-up-and-down clown. I'm just saying that you have to be very aware that people are watching.

A lot of times, what happens during the day rises or falls depending on how you carry yourself. So it's critical that you start the day correctly.

Work throughout the day to center your mind and stay focused on the right things:

- Honor people

- Advocate for high levels of integrity
- Be honest
- Build trust into your conversations

Then also help your team to have fun. It's very hard to do that if you're just a jacked-up mess.

Respect, honor, and dignity can come in lots of different packages.

It's up to you to figure out:

- How are you wired?
- How has God put you together?
- How can you lead well, with respect, honor, and dignity?

How I show honor, respect, and dignity to a team could be much different than how you do that, because God wired us differently. But if you're not focused on trying to figure out how that is, your leadership will be weak at best.

Live a Grace-Filled Life

People under my leadership have sometimes been caught off-guard because through the years, I've tried hard to show some grace and mercy. I've tried not to be overly judgmental on topics or issues.

I consistently try to have fun; not that I do it well all

the time, but I try. I try to be someone who does all the things that I'm promoting in this book. That doesn't mean that I do it successfully every day. I'm sure I mess up.

My wife tells me all the time, "Hey, you're not who you think you are."

Sometimes you can be working hard to be that kind of person. Then you get into a situation where someone just isn't performing. It's happened to me multiple times. You're having tough conversations with someone about their performance, and their ability to stay in the organization.

Maybe you have to confront their:

- Lack of performance
- Apathy about what's going on
- Wrong behaviors for your team

Then you have to approach them to tell them, "This isn't going to work. We're not going to allow this kind of behavior. You're not going to be able to stay here if you're behaving like this, or not performing."

Because you've worked so hard to be upbeat, to have a positive attitude, and not to be overly judgmental, your response to their actions and attitudes may come as a shock. While it's true that you are walking with the idea of showing grace if someone makes a mistake, you cannot be weak and let the team suffer because someone is not performing the way they need to.

You will have to make hard decisions. That doesn't mean that they have to be made in a mean and nasty way.

Even in the hard decisions, you can have grace, honor, and dignity toward the person, all the way through the process. I use the word *deselection*. It doesn't really exist as a word, but I think of myself as having to select and deselect people.

If someone is not performing, you have to deselect them. You have to relieve them from the organization. But it doesn't mean you don't like them. It doesn't mean that you don't think they're a great person. It just means that they're not performing, or they're not fitting in this organization or this team. You don't want to be weak about that, because it will adversely affect all of the organization.

The concepts of Grace and Judgment run in conflict to one another. They're in horrible contrast, but you can have both as a leader. It is a dichotomy because on one hand, you show grace; you are merciful. On the other hand, you have to make tough decisions and you have to protect the team; you have to remove people who are not contributing in a positive way.

It takes a ton of work to say, "I can show grace. People make mistakes; people don't do things perfectly all the time. People have crises in their lives that affect their performance, and I have to show grace in all of that. I have to understand all of that."

It can be very difficult, but it can be done with intentionality. If you work at it, you can do it much better than we do in a lot of cases.

It can also be so simple. Treat people the way you want to be treated. That's the way you want to carry yourself. Think about how you want someone to treat you with respect in your workplace.

It's the Biblical standard: "Do unto others as you want done to you."

You want to carry yourself the way you do when you're in that good place in your mind and you think: *This would be the right thing to do. It would be very good for the organization and for this person.*

It does take work, but it is possible.

YOU DON'T HAVE ALL THE ANSWERS

I have never met anyone who has all the answers. I've met many people who *think* they have all the answers. No one really has all the answers, other than maybe

Jesus Christ himself, and I still am perplexed by some of his answers! So I would just say you don't have them, I don't have them, but collectively as a team, we have a lot better answers.

A Team Can Help You Get the Answers

When I got into the New York operation I spoke about earlier in the book, I think that the organization was stupefied by what was happening there.

I found key players I thought could help me come up with good answers. We put a team of four to six people around a table.

We discussed:

- Communication issues
- Safety issues
- Relational issues
- Performance issues

We asked each other, "What do we do?"

Instead of trying to find experts from different parts of the country to help us, I sat down with the team who actually worked in the operation. It was a very diverse team—people from different cultures and different departments. They knew the problems and knew the fixes.

I had arrived only a few months earlier. I was trying to figure out the current conditions of the problems, but the people who *knew* what was going on were the people who were in the operations.

We called them together and gave them support in the form of:

- Structure
- Education
- Understanding
- Instruction in effective communication

Pretty soon the team and I were making great strides in fixing the conditions in the building. I taught them about barriers to communication and how to overcome them.

They made great improvements in:

- Performance
- Communication
- Teamwork

Conditions got better quickly. The rest of the organization—especially the corporate parts of the organization—were very surprised.

But the improvement came from this diverse team of people who knew the conditions in their operation. They knew how to make it a better operation, but they weren't overly educated in business or in management. So no one listened to them; no one had given them a chance to fix it. No one had assembled them as a team. They hadn't received tools or guidance or guardrails to work within.

As soon as we provided those elements, they became one of the best-performing parts of the organization compared to where they had been just two or three years earlier.

Strive for Diversity

If you have a diverse group of people who have different learning experiences and different life experiences, they're coming to the table from different angles.

To imagine what this is like, think about sitting in an auditorium seat and looking at the stage. You're looking straight ahead, at a concert for instance, and performers are playing and it's beautiful. Now imagine being one of the artists onstage looking out into the audience. Your perspective of that concert would be totally different. Now imagine you are the stage manager, watching from the wings, looking across the stage. Your perspective on that concert would be totally different from either of the others.

The same is true in business and life and leadership. If you can put together a very different, diverse group around a table on any given issue, they'll see it differently.

Your perspectives change as a result of seeing others' perspectives.

Your ability to affect things will be:

- Stronger
- Faster
- Better-equipped

You can use your one perspective from staring straight at the concert, or you can incorporate that in a wonderful way with totally different perspectives.

One of You Is Enough

I learned this concept from my wife.

Sometimes she'll say, "So, you're doing pretty good, huh? How are you doing?"

When I'm having fun with her and teasing her, I'll say, "If I was any better, I'd be twins!"

She'll say, "Oh no, no, no; the world can only take one of you!"

You really only need *one* of you. You need a team of people who are nothing like you.

Imagine being able to win a football game, but the only players that you have are defensive players. You can't score a point! You can stop the other team pretty well, but you can't score a point.

In business, the team has to have a diverse group of experiences and understanding, even education and learning, because that's what's going to bring you the best solutions. Including people with different understandings really helps a team perform at its top level. Find out about the different kinds of people in the organization.

What are the different skills they bring?

Gallup Strength Center has a great software program called StrengthsFinder. The program helps you look at your five top strengths and compare them with other team members' strengths. Nine times out of ten there are a lot of differences. You want to combine a variety of strengths in a mix.

An old buddy I used to work with liked to say that a good team is like a great stew; you just keep putting in different ingredients, and it tastes better and better. I think that's true for most good teams. You don't just make a stew of nothing but carrots; it wouldn't taste so good.

When you're processing, you really want to process

with the idea that, "I want different, I don't want the same. I'm not looking to build a cookie-cutter organization."

Just because God has given you a unique set of gifts doesn't mean that He hasn't given someone else a set of gifts. All people have talents and gifts. You want a good mixture. You don't want a whole team of CFOs; it's just not going to work.

Allowing different skills to surface from the group takes a bit of humility. Even though you may want to think that you and how you're wired is the best, it may be okay for you but not for someone else. You have to be humble enough to know there are a lot of great qualities in all kinds of people.

You have to be smart enough and humble enough:

- To look for diverse people
- To utilize their skills
- To let them fly and do their thing

Look for Diverse Ages

I'm fifty-five years old and I love to hang out with folks who are seventy-five or eighty. When I find people of that age who teach me about history and their life experiences, it's just a blast! They have been where I am going.

I also love hanging out with eighteen- to thirty-five-year-olds, because they're seeing the world through a different lens. They're bringing up ideas that I wouldn't have a clue about. They're teaching me things and helping me see the world through a new, fresh eye.

I like trying to find the other end of where I am. If you can find both ends, if you can get the experience of hanging out with people younger and older than you, it's fantastic.

It's a little more difficult if you're twenty-five and trying to find somebody who's younger than you. But I really believe that there's so much to be learned. There are many lessons about life and business to learn from seniors, if you're willing to learn. But there's just as many lessons to learn from someone who is young and full of energy, and full of life, trying to work it out, figure it out, and seeing it through a different lens.

Seniors will sometimes pooh-pooh the ideas of a young person just because they're young. That's a shame, because those elders are missing out. And young folks who dismiss older folks are missing out on the wisdom, understanding, and the richness of what they could learn and carry throughout the course of their lives.

Remember, you *need* other folks in your life. All humans are built for community; and community does not mean just people who are like you in age or outlook.

Another important piece to remember is that *you do not have all the answers.*

If you're a high-capacity leader and you think you have all the answers, you don't. Don't be confused.

If you do think you have all the answers, like my buddy Mark Wimms would say, "You just bumped your head."

So forget it! Really work to remind yourself that you do not have all the answers, and that's okay.

Someone will have the answers you don't. Search for them. Find them. Put them on your team.

You're going to be much better off for it.

CHAPTER

FOUR

Building a Better Process

TEAMWORK, TRUST, AND RELATIONSHIP

Teamwork is critical.

Often the team doesn't do so well because all we've done is name them as a team but we haven't given them any of the tools that they need to function well.

Without the right tools, the group won't function together. It just doesn't work. Then people are upset because the teams are just named a team but nothing more. They feel ineffective.

Be Intentional When Selecting the Team Members

In order to be intentional about selecting team members, you really have to know the team well.

You need to know:

- The players
- Their background
- Their education

- Their business or work background
- How they're wired

By now hopefully you've given them a few assessments that will help them understand their talent mix and their skill sets. Then when you're helping them to form that team, be intentional. Go for a balance of extroverts and introverts, for example, or aim for one engineer instead of five.

Really think through:

- *How much do I know in aligning this team?*
- *Whom do I want working together?*
- *What am I trying to build for the future?*

There's a lot to think about when you start forming a team to execute a project.

If you're working on a project in a particular department, you may need one or two people out of that department on that team. Let's just say you're working in operations, for instance. It may be very important to have someone from accounting, someone from human resources (HR), and someone from another part of the operation. That is going to give the team different perspectives, and it's going to educate other departments about what's really happening in your operation.

The same would be true if you were to start a project in HR. If you gather people from accounting, operations, and purchasing, when you pull those members together, there's a higher degree of perspectives coming into the discussion. There's also learning going on about that department.

Giving people from different departments the chance to work together helps build continuity and builds trust in the organization because now people know each other better. They know what the department does. They have a little bit more insight, which helps them become better at their jobs.

We Are All at the Same Level; All Opinions Count

Some teams have different levels, or a hierarchy. The problem with that arrangement is that there's a tendency for everyone to defer to the leader. Leave your hat outside the room — leave your title outside as well.

If you're the manager and you have a couple of administrators working with you, or if you're a higher-level vice president, for instance, you need to leave your title or your hat outside the room. You need to show people that their opinions are just as valued, no matter their level in the workplace. They can't defer to you as the leader on what you're all going to do. That's not going to create the best result.

The team needs to understand that when you all get

into the room and work on the project, there is no boss. There is only all of you together, and all of you bring value. Each person brings a different perspective, and each one is needed.

Another way to plan for success is to make sure that each person around that table has a job:

- If someone's very good at taking notes, then make them the scribe or recorder.

- If someone is very good at arranging information, then they're the organizer.

- If you're working on an HR project and someone knows the law, then they can be the law resource.

But not one of them is the boss. No one person is the end-all, be-all, and they don't make the final decision.

The team makes the decision.

When building high-performance teams, you have to have a facilitator: someone who's not necessarily directly connected to the team at that moment. When you train your organization on how to be a high-performing team, explain to them that these kinds of questions have to come up. They have to be vetted out, or explained to the team, or it won't go well.

Build Strategic Relationships in Your Organization

I have experience in manufacturing and distribution; that's where most of my experience lies. I would say that if you use the manufacturing environment as an example, in that environment you could have ten to fifteen different departments.

There might be:

- A maintenance department
- A cutting department
- A preparation department
- An assembly department
- All kinds of sub-departments throughout your facility

As the leader, you will probably be able to sense when one department isn't connected to another in the way that you'd like it to be. You can make sure to include an appropriate mix of department members on the team.

Perhaps you're thinking: *The distribution arm doesn't understand really how this product is coming out of manufacturing. I want to make sure I have someone out of that distribution department in this project.*

You're really thinking hard as a leader, not just about what you're trying to execute to improve this process or this piece of the organization.

What relationships are you trying to build?

Who could teach another perspective?

There may also be a lack of understanding about how preparation works, for instance. Well, then, it may be very important for you as you build teams to make sure one preparation department team member is on just about every team, because of the lack of understanding and knowledge about preparation. They'll bring that to the team.

You're not just thinking: *I need these five people to do this and this.* You're thinking deeper and wider.

You are asking bigger questions like:

- *How is it going to affect me today?*
- *How is it going to affect me tomorrow?*
- *How is it going to affect me two years from now?*

You're really thinking strategically now.

Where are you going, and how are you going to get there?

Who needs to build relationships with whom as you work on the projects?

Trust

When you assemble this team, hopefully you personally

have created a sense of trust with the organization as a leader.

Ask yourself: *What could we do to create some trust in each other as a team before we take off?*

You can do this in a fun way. Keep the objective in mind, and then think of the craziest, funniest, most interesting team names you can come up with.

Some teams I've worked with have tried to build a song around their name. People laugh and have fun while they're brainstorming the names. Then they vote. Voting on the top three or four names seems to pull the group together; they start to feel that they are a real team. They've already started to form some trust, because the boss or the perceived leader didn't get to pick the team name, the team did. That's a little thing that you can do for your team at the beginning to really build trust, right out of the gate.

TEN STEPS FOR SUCCESS

Whether your organization is made up of twenty-five or seventy-five people, if you don't start to build a systematic approach to how to work on projects, nothing will get really solidified.

When teams come together and work on projects, these ten steps will:

- Have meaning
- Give definition to the project
- Be purposeful

Without them, everyone just brings their own opinion to the game.

With them, you and the teams can decide thing like:

How will you go about making improvements?

How will you function as a team?

Remember:

- Don't skip steps.
- Don't try to change them.
- Follow the process.

Ninety-nine percent of the time, if you follow this process, you're going to have a wonderful outcome. I know this from experience. Your outcome is going to be way better than any you've ever had before.

The process I'm giving you will help you have a much better outcome and deliverable. As well, you'll get a much better finish to your project than you would have had otherwise.

Step 1: Define the Objective

You or the organization has discovered something that

needs to be fixed—especially in the beginning. You *identify* the problem. You have to know and define what you want to complete. You also need to make sure that everyone's aligned on the objectives and they understand the end goal.

Any time you tackle a project, there's a potential for *scope creep*. Scope creep is when you start off trying to solve a little problem—let's say you're making a handle for some kind of fashion bag. The stitching in that handle is always a problem, and it impacts the way you paint the handle.

If you don't keep in mind the clearly defined end goal or objective that you're fixing the handle, you might take a step back and end up fixing the whole bag *and* the two bags alongside of it that you're producing. You'll have all kinds of scope creep and you'll never complete the project.

To prevent scope creep:

- Be specific about the goal
- Nail it down
- Stay true to it

Defining and sticking to the objective is very important to the process.

The process starts with knowing the objective.

Step 2: Pick the Team

You want to pull together a diverse team of people from different departments or skill sets within the organization. Four or five people together works well. At maximum, you'd want six to eight people. With this number, every team member has an important role to play.

Step 3: Build Trust in the Team

Just like in the team-naming activity described above, you want to make sure all team members feel:

- At ease
- Supported
- Listened to
- They are important members of an interconnected group

You need people to feel free to make suggestions and to offer and receive feedback. Trust is critical in creating the right atmosphere to allow the best work to come forward.

Step 4: Study All Current Conditions

Here is where you dig deep into the objective or what needs to be fixed. You study all of the current conditions that you can possibly think of. Help the team make a list of those conditions.

Ask:

"What is happening right now?"

"What's going on today?"

Listing the current conditions will give you important information for understanding the problem and ways of fixing it.

Step 5: Analyze the Root Cause

Once you've established the list of current conditions, look at it with your team.

Where do you notice gaps?

What's the root cause of your conditions–good, bad, or indifferent?

Step 6: Create Countermeasures

This is the time to put some countermeasures in place to try to hit your objective. You have the clearly defined objective in place, you have the creative minds thinking together, now you try out your ideas for how to achieve the goal.

So you create the countermeasure and put it in place. You try something; you test something.

Countermeasures sometimes work and sometimes

they don't work. So you might need to keep trying different ones.

Step 7: Test Countermeasures

After countermeasures are complete you need to know whether you've achieved your goal. If you have achieved it, then you know you can go on to teach this to others.

If you didn't achieve what you wanted, you need to talk about what is the root cause of the problem.

You need to do more testing, more assessing, and perhaps come up with new countermeasures. Through this process of testing and assessing, you will find the right solution. Keep at it until you find what works.

Step 8: Ensure New Gains Are Sustainable

Now that you've got your solution, you need to figure out how to keep it going. You need to return to the situation and check it in two weeks, in three months, in four months, and continuing.

Are people following your guidelines?

Is the process continuing to work?

In other words, Step Eight is follow-up.

Step 9: Sharing Results

Now that you know your plan works, you need to present it to the rest of the organization, to the people who are riding with you. You're going to teach them what you've discovered and show them the way.

You're going to share:

- What you have learned
- What works
- Any other areas you found as part of the process that might need fixing
- What you would push for
- Recommendations for the next project

Step 10: Document the Project

The final step is making sure that your findings are visible somewhere in the organization so you don't forget the project. Documentation also allows the team to speak the same language when working on a project.

You'll want to write standard operating procedures. This could be a simple list of how-tos, so others can easily repeat your steps. You want to put visual controls up somewhere, so people know the new way you have found, the easiest way, to do something. Usually it's best to create a one-page document so you can post it for the whole world to see: "Team ABC did this project on this date, and it was a great success."

These steps are not the same for every project, because some projects are different. However, the process should stay fairly consistent.

HOW TO MAKE THIS STUFF STICK

Sustainability is one of the hardest struggles that organizations have. You can do a project and have a wonderful team and the team is ecstatic about their work! But unless you put some really strong effort into making it stick, you'll come back three months later and everything that the team put together is gone.

Because people have common knowledge, they go back to what they've always known. They infuse their own opinions about how it should go and what should happen, but they weren't on a team that spent forty hours or fifty hours trying to define this process and really make it work.

People not on the team may believe that they have a better way. They make an adjustment, and that adjustment turns into another adjustment, and another adjustment. Three or four months later, you come back and uh-oh! Lo and behold, your team's recommendations have gotten lost. You put all that work into it and it's already gone. So this piece is pretty important and it's very difficult to ensure that it stays.

Stay True to the Process

Define the process and stay true to it. If you don't, there's no way to know whether it worked or not. You won't know how to enhance the process, so you can't build upon it. You won't have a chance to make it better and better for your organization, because you never really started with locking down the process.

That's really critical for the team.

It's critical for the organization.

It's critical for your success.

Celebrate the Gains and Wins

Find places all along the process to celebrate the wins.

You start by understanding the key objective. Define the key objective so you all know. And when you do that, celebrate the fact that everyone understands clearly that you all know where you're going, what you're trying to work on.

You know the objectives. You're ready to work on naming the team. When you've named the team, celebrate the win!

There's a great book by Malcolm Gladwell called *The Tipping Point*. The idea is that by celebrating these wins all along the way, until you tip over the edge, and now you have the momentum you want as an organization, as a team.

Many organizations are fantastically critical about getting better and better. This is important, but they don't take just a minute to celebrate, to acknowledge the win, celebrate for a second, and then move on.

When you celebrate the wins, you:

- Build momentum
- Build credibility
- Build trust
- Build respect

Take that moment to say, "Good job! You got that. Let's go to the next thing."

This builds energy. Don't wait until the very end of the project when everybody is worn out and tired to celebrate. By that time, everybody will be exhausted! Waiting until the end drains energy.

Having Engagement at all Levels in the Organization

Former U.S. Secretary of State Colin Powell did a wonderful presentation on leadership and there are several versions of slideshows online based on his talk.

If you haven't seen any of them, Google it, and look at all of the slides.

One of his key points is, "Don't trust the experts."

What does he mean by that?

Let's say you're going to work on a project, and you decide that only managers are going to be allowed to work on this project even though it's going to affect all kinds of pieces of the organization.

The management team comes in. There are two or three engineers and there are two or three grad students. They work on a project that we'll say is going to be in your distribution operation. The team does a wonderful job.

They learn all kinds of things. They make all kinds of changes.

They tell the people who work there every day, "This is what you're going to do. This is how you're going to do it, because we have discovered the best way."

Then the expert team members go back to their offices, wherever, and they go back to their work.

The workers—the people who are actually doing the work the experts told them to—think the new way is a joke.

They complain, "These people who are experts, who

are supposed to have all the brains, came down here and they don't have a clue what we do or how we do it. They expect us to do it the way they told us to. We know that's never going to work. They don't realize that's never going to work."

But they just allow that team to go away, and within days, they just go back to doing it the way they've always done it.

That's why it's so important to make sure that you have team members from every level of the organization intimately involved in your project.

If your project is in the maintenance department, part of that team has to be made up of maintenance members.

If you're working on an accounting issue, part of the team has to be from accounting.

If the work affects HR, part of the team has to be the people who do that work every day.

It cannot be a group of elitists who come in. It's wonderful to have engineers and high-level managers in your organization. It's okay to have one or two of them on your team, maybe even three, but if you're not careful, the people who have to do the work every day aren't going to be able to execute the experts' plan.

The team needs people who:

- Are from the department
- Are invested
- Have ownership in that department or that situation

Create a Simple Standard Operating Procedure

In my career, I've been very involved in making what I would consider one of the best vehicles in the world, and I've also had the great opportunity of working with what I would consider is one of the best luxury products in the world. We have worked on wonderful projects, and all kinds of new systems that enhanced operations, but we could always boil down that enhancement with a simple *standard operating procedure*, or SOP.

For example, let's say it takes seven steps to doing something.

The SOP should be:

- Simple
- Bulleted, not chapters of information
- Posted at the worksite

When people are doing their work, they should be able to look up and see the steps. They should also be able to feel that they created those steps with their team and know it's the best way. The SOP is a reminder for the workers who are in it every day, moving around from station to station. It's a simple, basic reminder: do these seven things.

A standard operating procedure makes your process better and better. You can analyze it.

Is it working?

Is it really giving you what you want?

If it's not, you can adjust it.

Visual Management Controls

The best examples of visual management controls can be found in and around many airports throughout the world.

On the highway going to the airport, there's usually a sign, or visual management, that says, "Rental cars go here, drop-offs go here, arrivals go here."

The visual management tells you at every step of your approach:

- Where to go
- What to do
- When to do it
- How to do it

This goes on all the way down to your gate, your seat,

whether you're at the window or the aisle. They're all visual controls. No one has to tell you; you can just look up and get to the next thing if you know anything about traveling.

The same thing holds true for your organization. Wherever you can have visual controls, put them in place.

When I walk into the front door of your organization, when I get into the parking lot, where do I go?

I can't tell you how many company parking lots I've driven into and I don't have a clue where the front door is!

I find it, but there's no visual control that says, "Main Office, Administration, Information."

Then in the hallway someone gives the direction that "Bob's on the right."

Well then I feel like a little rat in a maze: "Where is Bob?"

Then as it turns out, there are three Bobs, so which Bob do I want?

So I think the best example of great visual management — some of the best examples — are airports. But believe me, if you can do that in your organization, it's a huge win.

It's going to make you way more efficient.

It's going to simplify what's going on every day.

Visitors, new hires; all have an easier time moving forward to understand how this organization works and where things are located.

It's really critical in manufacturing. There are many issues that require visual tools to keep people healthy and safe.

CHAPTER
FIVE

Taking Care of Your Top Three
(Customer, Team, and Company)

WHY YOU HAVE TO CARE

I have run into multiple managers and leaders who have never developed the skill of caring for their team. They're practitioners, so they know how to manage, they know how to lead very well, but they don't necessarily understand that they have to care, truly care, about the team that they're working with.

Leaders need to care about:

- The team
- The whole company
- The customers

A lot of people exit school or basic management and leadership training and stop at being a practitioner. They just practice what they've learned in school. They don't have an understanding that they have to have a zeal for the people. This is critical. Sometimes people just miss it.

Think of Your Company as a Living, Breathing Organism

I think that this idea could run both for a manager and for a leader or entrepreneur. Your first question was around the idea that you have to care, and the second question is more wrapped around the idea that you're developing a living, breathing organism.

When you start a company, if you're an entrepreneur, you have this passion, you have this zeal inside of you to perform and to add value and to bring something that is going to generate revenue and is going to do some good things for a lot of people, or you wouldn't do it. So you have that passion inside of you.

Over time, if you're very successful, you could grow to a place where you aren't intimately involved anymore, and you don't realize that the team that you've put together under you has stopped caring, or they just don't have a passion for the business the way you do.

It's like a birthing process. You're birthing something new if you're an entrepreneur. You've birthed this brand new baby and you want to take care of it. You want it to grow; you want to nurture it. If you're a manager or leader in an organization, and you're taking over responsibility, it's almost like an adoption process. You've adopted ownership of this child, if you will, or this living, breathing thing.

If you can keep these concepts firmly in your head and keep coming back to them, I think that your success rate goes up, because you're nurturing a piece of yourself. The organization is a part of you.

If you don't care about it, it loses its life, passion, and creativity.

To me starting a company or organization has always felt like I was adopting it:

- I cared deeply about its success.
- I cared about its health.
- I cared about what was happening within it.

Whetheryouarecominginandtakingoverresponsibility, or you've actually birthed an organization yourself, the closest thing that comes to it in my mind is parenting.

You wouldn't let your child just run amok. You wouldn't let someone else just take care of it. I've seen a lot of cases where owners got very successful, and then they become absentee owners. They're there physically, but their mind isn't there, they're not engaged the way they used to be, they're not intimately involved in the business, and then they wonder why it starts to slip.

It's All About People

People are built for community. They are built for connectedness. There are no successful companies without people (that I know of). I think that the companies who have done this connection between people and their products at the highest levels have the greatest amount of success.

Look at a company like Starbucks. They built a sense of community. When you walk into their facility, it feels like you're home; it's that sense of community.

Look at a company like Apple. They have built a product that has created easier ways to connect with people, easier ways to build a sense of community, if you would.

Those organizations have intentionally stayed connected to their team. Starbucks gives their team members benefits that are very, very good. Apple has built its team around their products. It's just very interesting and you can't get away from it.

Some of us who are a little older may say social media are not really community. But a lot of our younger generations would say it is; it's how they stay connected and know what's going on.

I worked for Toyota for twenty-six years, and we went full circle: At one point we were trying to use more and more robotics, but over time, it just didn't work as well as having real, live humans interacting with the machinery itself. The nimbleness, the ability to look at the product and to understand what the customer is seeing, it can't happen with a robot or a computer. It can only happen with physical people.

No organization is going to go very far without people. You're certainly not going to develop a great organization without your customer.

Caring About the Customer

Care enough about your customer to know that you're either enhancing their life or you're causing conflict or stress in their life. You're fulfilling a need. Someone is bringing their hard-earned money so you can meet a need, or facilitate their journey through life. you're either going to improve their journey or negatively impact their journey.

The same is true for caring about your team members. You need to care about them more than the union does.

A lot of times, organizations lose sight of the fact that they're negatively impacting their customer or their team member. It's often the case that when you make a phone call into an organization, especially if the organization is large, it could take a very long time to get to living, breathing person.

Every friend, anybody that I've talked to wants that: to reach another human. They're clicking, clicking, clicking; they're hitting star-three, four, five, hitting zero for operator, because they're just looking for a living, breathing person to talk to.

Why?

Why not listen to the computer and answer the questions that the computer asks?

Because people are looking to connect with someone who can relate to their issue, not just answer the question for them. Most of the time it's a relatability issue. Customers deserve great service.

Do whatever you have to do to take care of your customer.

Team members deserve leaders and managers who build:

- A sense of community
- A sense that everyone does all they can to support each other
- A sense that everyone does all they can to support the products they build

You need to understand that your customer has worked like crazy to produce revenue to go buy your product or your service. If you mess it up, then you're negatively impacting them after they've already been impacted by having to make the money to buy your product. It becomes a double-whammy. They worked really hard to earn that income, and now they're kind of stuck with the fact that they put their money into something that has not been a great experience. Worse yet, they may conclude that they bought your service and you don't even care about it.

I ran an operation in New York that was a union operation. When I arrived there, the union truly cared more about the team on the floor and in the operation than the management team that I was working with did. As we started to shift gears, it became clear that we had a new team with a new leader who really cared about them and their work.

Then, all of the sudden, the game started to change for the team. They realized that the company wasn't just out for itself. They understood that someone leading that piece of the organization didn't care like they should have.

Over time, we built great relationships, we were able to affect change, and pretty soon, the team that had the union representing them decertified that union and went on to do great things in the organization. They shifted their mindset from believing an outside organization has to come in and care for your team, and represent your team, because you don't care and you won't represent your team.

I'm not saying all managers are that way, or that every condition is that way. I think there are plenty of times where a union makes a lot of sense and adds a lot of value. But there are many times that the union is only there because the organization lost its way.

They turn to the union so someone will:

- Care for the team
- Represent the team
- Care about them as much as the company

This is always a tricky balancing act, but it's one that needs to be worked through, and you need to be very intentional about the fact that the team who is producing the product or representing the product is just as valuable as the people who buy the product.

If you are an entrepreneur, or if you are a leader or manager in an organization, and you have team members who don't care, it is up to you to take the time to help them rediscover the necessity to care for the team and the organization and the customer. If they do not, then it's time to remove them from the organization and let them be blessed into something new, because they've just lost their way with you and your team.

If you leave them in it, you're not doing any favors:

- For yourself
- For the rest of the team
- For the customers

Letting them go doesn't have to be a horrible, mean, nasty fight; it needs to be just an honest dialogue that acknowledges that for whatever reason, they are not enjoying what they're doing any longer, and it's time for them to find something else.

Don't be afraid to make those decisions. The times when it's necessary to be upset or angry to separate someone from the company are exceptional.

Usually, I sit down with someone after many long conversations to tell them, "You and I both know it's just not working. I care deeply about you. I care about our customers. We have to figure out a way that you can move on and do some other things."

TAKING A GENUINE INTEREST IN HOW THINGS WORK INSIDE OF YOUR COMPANY

Sometimes it can feel difficult to spend time out in the operation, in different departments, discovering what people are up against, discovering what's working and what's not working. But it's critical to the process. Even in organizations of upwards of three or four hundred people on the floor, you need to get to know people.

Try to spend a little bit of time with every team member in the first few months of your time in that operation. You will discover obstacles your teams face and what people are working on. Sometimes you'll learn about things that are very painful, and sometimes things that are very exciting.

When you take this time, you get to know the business. If your business is growing like crazy, it's hard to keep track of all the pieces of it. So take the time to get out in the operation, or to get inside of the departments — whether it's an information technology department or an HR department — and really discover what people are up against.

You can make their lives so much easier and so much more productive with a few tweaks, with a few removing of obstacles, that they have no ability to change, or to do anything about. They're just there, doing their task all day long. Most of the time, they also can tell you how to do it better!

They can say to you, "If we just had this little tool, or this little piece, or if we had this kind of information, we could be so much more effective, and no one's taken the time to listen to that."

It's really important that you are the kind of person who is pressing the flesh. It's almost like you're a little politician in your own organization. You're out shaking hands, you're talking to people, you're genuinely interested in what's happening with them, and you genuinely care what they're up against.

Understand the Obstacles so You Can Help Remove Them

As you spend time out on the floor or getting to meet people throughout the company, you'll start to see:

- Issues
- Obstacles
- Disconnects
- Inefficiencies

If you have free reign to go into any operation on any given day and look at it, work in it, spend some time with people, you can bring useful information to any department that will help them create change.

Let's say you're in a marketing division. There are five or six people inside your marketing department. They work very hard all day, every day, trying to organize marketing, and trying to put the marketing plan together.

Yesterday, you just happened to be at a retail store,

a place where marketing never really goes because they're stuck in their offices working on whatever they're working on. You can bring information from the retail store to the marketing division.

It could change what's happening in the marketing arena, because you get to see things that they don't. That's how you start removing obstacles. You know things; hopefully you've seen things or you're pushing yourself to know things and see things. You're going to be able to use them to enhance your team.

If you want only to run operations, without getting involved in HR or any other departments, then you're limiting your ability to really help your team. Sometimes it's obvious. HR just needs the tool that you've known about for three years, and once you're in there alongside of them for a couple of hours discovering what they do, you can simply suggest purchasing the tool to help them get to the next level of efficiency.

Hopefully you've visited other kinds of organizations that are like yours and discovered better or different tools. Finding best practices will be key for your team. Then you can help them move forward.

It's critical as a leader that you always look for best practices. You're always looking for the things that are going to make your organization and your team more efficient. If you're not doing it, no one else will. If you are doing it, everyone else will.

You could even passionately make that a part of what you expect out of your team, meaning that you could say, "I expect my team to leave this facility twice a year and go see a best practice somewhere, and then come back and implement those best practices in our organization."

You can dictate that because you're the leader! If you don't do it, no one else will.

It's a never-ending battle. You could remove obstacles this month, and come back and have brand new obstacles next month. You could implement a practice and in a few months you might have to adjust it again. If you're not consistently looking for the obstacles and you're not consistently in your operations, you will come back a year later and wonder what happened. A year is too long.

You're There to Make the Team's Job Easier, Not Harder

In earlier chapters we talked about communications. You have to be a good communicator and be willing to communicate over and over again. Sometimes people think the leader is there to make them work harder.

Typically, workers think the company's motivation is more:

- Production
- Efficiency
- Money

You have to be communicating with your team about your real purpose for being there, which is to help them discover a better way forward.

You're looking for new ways to allow the workers to expend less energy and produce more products, or get better tools to produce better documents.

Chapter Four outlines how to set up an environment focused on continuous improvement in your organization. Refer to that chapter for more about putting together effective teams. You are really trying to discover how to become more and more efficient and help the team know that efficiency and productivity are your goals.

It's not about making them work harder and breaking their backs in the process. It's about working their brains.

The Difference Between "Busy" and "Productive"

So many team members will say, "I'm so busy. I'm

working like crazy. I get here at six o'clock in the morning, and I'm here until six o'clock at night."

That's really good, but it's not as good as being productive.

Productivity sounds more like when someone says, "I'm using every moment to build value and to move forward. I'm not doing work that I'm going to have to rework later."

You don't want people doing work that isn't adding value now. It could potentially add value a week from now, but then again it may never add value.

You may hear someone say, "As long as I stay busy, as long as when the boss comes around I stay busy, then everyone will be happy."

You don't want your teams feeling or thinking that way.

You want them thinking: *I really want to be productive, and move every initiative forward. I want to be in forward progress; not moving side-to-side, not going backwards and then coming forward, but moving forward and straight ahead.*

You need to communicate that to the team. You need to show them how and help them discover that doing tons of busywork isn't necessarily helping the company. It won't help them either.

Like I said before, I spent a lot of years in Toyota.

In the late 1980s and early 1990s we would tell team members, "If your assigned task is done, just have a seat in this chair. Sit down and wait for the next task. Don't think you have to do a bunch of things between the tasks."

Imagine that you're producing some kind of product, and you can do busywork. Let's say we're making brake housings for a vehicle, and I've made all the brake components I need to make for the day or for the hour, and I just keep producing more and more and more.

Then we find out an hour or two later that the customer's demand has stopped and I have overproduced by a hundred. Now the company has to throw those away. I was busy, but it wasn't productive—because all the extra components were tossed away.

You want to make sure that you are producing and moving forward what you need and how you need it. That's much more valuable than being busy.

You have to be able to help the team see that staying busy isn't adding value now, and it may not add value later.

The Next Customer in Line

Whatever the workers in a process do, you want to make sure they hand the material to the next person inside of the business as if that next person were a customer. Let's say they're working in HR, and you have to produce a newsletter that's going to the team members in operations. You want to produce that newsletter and hand it to the operators. And they will hand it to the staff in the best working order that they can: professional, articulate, well written, so that it can be delivered to the rest of the team in a very efficient manner.

The same would be true in a production environment. If you are working in a department that is cutting widgets for a product, but the cut is off just by an eighth of an inch, and the next team has to sand down the eighth of an inch just to use the product, they didn't really think about my next customer in line. If you cut the product perfectly and hand it to the next customer in line who's going to use that widget, then their job is that much more efficient.

And if they hand it to the person who's going to put those four pieces together, then that job is more efficient.

We think about the end customer — the retail customer — many times, but we don't usually think: *Everything that*

I do as a worker is negatively or positively affecting other workers through this supply chain.

Let's say you and I are working together, and I'm handing you products to work with for the next step in production. So if I hand it to you, the next customer in line, perfectly, your job's much, much easier. If I hand it to you just a little bit off, it negatively impacts your job.

What we want to be talking about to our team is, you're not just worried about the retail customer, you're worried about the next customer in line beside you.

Then when you produce the final product, what is it?

It's perfect, because everyone along the supply chain made sure that they did their job absolutely as well as they could, because they were thinking about the next customer, or fellow worker in line, not just the retail customer.

CARING FOR THE WHOLE PERSON

Early in my career, people made time for me. I mentioned Dave Sloan before. He took time to care about how I was living mentally. He took time to teach me, coach me, and push me toward more education. He truly, genuinely cared about who we were as a team, and what we were trying to do. It showed up not just in our work, but in everything that was happening around us.

The time Dave spent in mentoring me is such a big part of whatever success I've had in my career. If I hadn't had people like him around me, I don't think I would be anywhere near where I am today. That's why I feel so strongly that caring for people is important.

Health

If your team is not mentally and physically healthy then they're not producing their best products. They're not taking care of their customers as well as they could. They're not serving anyone.

In your leadership role you might feel that others' health is not your problem. It probably isn't your personal problem, but it is your job to pay attention it. You can affect how healthy the team is going to be, and how well they're going to take care of themselves.

When I worked with Toyota it was a big organization. They had staffs of six or seven hundred people in a building. It was huge! They had health departments, and the nurse at my building was very good at making sure that people were physically in good shape. They had not only healthy working conditions, but also healthy ways of taking care of and exercising their bodies.

I know it's going to sound crazy for Americans, but at Toyota, we exercised every morning. We stretched; we did a little bit of dancing—if you could call it dancing. It was just a fun way to get ourselves revved up in the morning, get loose before we physically started to work. So your physical health is critical. You can manifest that in your organization however you like, but it's important for you as a leader to take it into consideration.

Education

Education should never end. I've worked with people who got their doctorate degree in 1990, but they haven't learned anything since then. Once they got their degree, they were done and their education stopped.

Be a lifelong learner. I think that once you can get yourself in the position of lifelong learning, then you can get your team into position for lifelong learning. This is how you will stay relevant and successful throughout the history of your work.

You have to continue to take time to educate yourself. There are constantly new ideas, practices, and concepts.

Our companies are changing, and the reason our companies are changing is because every couple of years, a new generation is coming into an organization with:

- New ideas
- New desires
- New expectations
- New experiences

You don't want to be Oldsmobile. Oldsmobile's customers died and their product died with them, because they weren't consistently educating themselves and their teams.

I personally am the product of a system that allowed me to go from less than a high school education to at least what I would consider a bachelor's or a master's degree in business.

Be that kind of organization.

Be that kind of leader.

Meet your team where they are.

If they're all hovering somewhere around eighth- or ninth-grade education level, then start teaching them from that level and move them forward. If they're all higher than that, start higher than that and move them forward. But for goodness sake, don't leave them where you find them!

Safety

It only takes one or two accidents in an organization

for you to come to grips with the fact that you are responsible for the team's safety. You have to develop ways to enhance the safety culture in which you live. I'm not talking about making it so litigious or so rule-oriented that nobody can move left or right, or so they're bound in bubble-wrap so they don't get hurt. I'm talking about creating environments and cultures in which people or conscious of safety all the time.

Have you ever heard of a near-miss?

Instead of waiting for an accident to happen in your organization, you develop a culture that supports filing an accident report even when there's *almost* an accident, when there's a near miss.

You require any team member in the organization to fill out a near-miss form that reports the almost-accident. Then you start investigating like it's a real accident. You fix all of the issues that you see. Take the time to fix whatever it is that you find.

It takes time and energy, but you can create the culture to investigate before someone is seriously injured. That will prevent accidents over the long haul.

Work-Life Balance

If you're lucky, life is a marathon. It's not a sprint.

If you don't have balance in your life, when you look back on it, it's either going to be short because you went too hard in one direction and you're either physically or mentally a mess, or you've bastardized your life in such a way that there's some aspect of life that's just disconnected.

We all know the great executives, men and women, who have risen to great heights in their organizations. Their families, their husbands and wives, are either a mess or are nonexistent, or they've gone through three or four marriages. Their kids are in trouble because the parent is not living a balanced life.

Many times, workers hope to please the boss, so they work twelve-hour days, seven days a week.

You need to be the leader or a manager who is willing to say to your team, "Enough's enough. I'm not proud of you working too long."

Work for the whole health of your team member.

If you're excited over twelve-hour days, fourteen-hour days, seven days a week, then you're creating a mess for your team, and you're probably going to create a mess for their lives. They're not going to be happy when they look back.

Realize it's a marathon.

Create that balance with:

- A good, strong work day
- Home time with your family
- Time to enjoy exercise
- Proper rest

Don't look at it as a sprint. It is a marathon.

It is a joy to see people grow and develop, to see people move throughout their life in a good, positive direction. You can look back on those team members and have a sense of fulfillment and gratification that you had a positive impact and influence on what they had to do. I could mention dozens of people who have been doing that for me throughout my life. Any time I've talked to them and thanked them for what they've done, they seem to be more excited about my success than I am!

You can look forward to a life where you have people saying to you, "Thank you so much for your time and energy and what you've done for me."

It's a gift that you're giving to people when you're a leader or a manager; you receive the gift of leading them or running your own organization.

The gift that you get to give back is caring deeply about people, and the influence and impact that you can have.

Conclusion

I hope that you are already on a journey of good leadership. I pray that this book gives you a new tool or two or maybe just a reminder. I hope that you will truly embrace it and enjoy it. May you have a wonderful journey of leadership throughout your life, whether that's within your family, within your work, within your church, or within your community.

My hope and prayer for you is that you consistently look for the next step in the journey. That may be in your own ability to learn new things. Maybe that means you'll find the next book that you want to read to inform new curriculum you want to implement with your team.

Reading this book has to be just the beginning or midway point. The journey should continue until the end of your life; at no point along that journey should you stop learning about leadership and how to lead and how to manage well, and how to care for folks the way you should.

My gift to you is sharing the thirty-plus years of experience that I've had in leadership.

Since retiring from Toyota in 2006, Ron has worked with and coached many senior leaders and owners of mutable companies. He has also been co-owner of three organizations.